Original title:
Camellia Chronicles

Copyright © 2025 Creative Arts Management OÜ
All rights reserved.

Author: Evelyn Hartman
ISBN HARDBACK: 978-1-80566-690-5
ISBN PAPERBACK: 978-1-80566-975-3

Waking Dreams Among Flora

In gardens where the blooms do giggle,
The bees in tuxedos start to wiggle.
Petals play hide and seek all day,
As butterflies laugh in a bright ballet.

Daisies weave tales of mischief and cheer,
While daisies discuss gossip with a deer.
The roses complain of a fragrance clash,
As laughter erupts with a playful splash.

A squirrel in shades, like a star on the rise,
Tells the lilies jokes that flip the skies.
The sunflowers nod with their heads held high,
As clouds poke fun, floating merrily by.

In this wild world where colors collide,
Every leaf holds a secret to confide.
So join the parade, let your worries cease,
In the land where flowers release their peace.

Beneath the Coral Canopy

Underneath the coral tree,
A squirrel danced with glee.
He wore a hat quite tall,
And tripped before us all.

The flowers giggled bright,
As color took to flight.
The bees began to hum,
To the beat of his bum.

A snail with flair joined in,
Spinning round like he'd win.
The grasshoppers stood still,
With hopes to get a thrill.

So here's to silly sights,
Where giggles blend with heights.
Beneath the coral sway,
We played the day away.

Secrets in Bloom

Petals whisper little dreams,
Of cookies and of ice cream.
The daisies made a pact,
To hide the funniest act.

A rose, with cheeky pride,
Wished to burst and glide.
While tulips tossed a joke,
And laughed till petals broke.

The garden's secret stash,
Of laughter, quite a cache.
A dandelion flew high,
With giggles as it flew by.

In this patch of mirth,
We find the lightest worth.
Where secrets bloom and blend,
Our joy will never end.

Echoes of the Garden

The garden hums a tune,
As cheeky frogs croak soon.
Sunflowers raise a brow,
To wonder, "Where's the cow?"

With winks and silly grins,
The plants play all their wins.
A cactus tells a tale,
Of hijinks on the trail.

Amidst the fragrant air,
A hedgehog took a dare.
To wear a flower crown,
And waddle round the town.

Echoes burst with delight,
In colors bold and bright.
In this whimsical land,
Laughter's always at hand.

The Language of Flowers

They say blooms speak their mind,
With secrets hard to find.
A daffodil once swore,
To make the tulip roar.

With petal tweets and sighs,
They whispered silly lies.
A violet made a jest,
And put the rose to rest.

The daisies locked a grin,
As happy bees buzzed in.
They danced the day away,
In this flower cabaret.

Words bloomed like fragrant cheer,
In gardens full of glee here.
Each laughter, bloom, and sound,
Turns nature upside down.

Threads of Time in Full Bloom

In the garden, time spins round,
A flower jokes without a sound.
Petals flicker like a smile,
Blooming antics all the while.

Bees are buzzing, sipping tea,
While snails race with utmost glee.
A worm wears shades, oh what a sight,
While daisies dance into the night.

With laughter wrapped in leafy dress,
The flowers all conspire to mess.
A climbing vine plays peek-a-boo,
While sunlight bathes in morning dew.

Threads of laughter in the breeze,
Nature's winks with perfect ease.
Here's to blooms that love to jest,
In a garden, we are blessed.

Portraits of Petal and Leaf

Petals pose for portraits bright,
Leaves twirl in their leafy flight.
A rose is striking a grand pose,
While tulips giggle, who knows?

Dandelions with crowns of fluff,
Claim royalty; that's their stuff.
Sunflowers wink with golden rays,
Spinning tales of sunny days.

Cacti roll their spiky eyes,
As they share their prickly lies.
In this gallery of green,
Laughter blooms like a well-kept dream.

With every color, joy unfolds,
A canvas bright that never molds.
In this botanical artful spree,
Every petal shouts, "Look at me!"

Moonlit Serenade in the Garden

Under the moon, the flowers hum,
Crickets play a merry drum.
Sleepy petals sway and dip,
As stars pour laughter from their trip.

Roses blush in silver light,
While daisies giggle at the sight.
The moon, with a grin, takes a seat,
As night unfolds its fragrant treat.

Mice in tuxedos dance on grass,
While shadows play their merry pass.
All is fun, in cosmic show,
In the garden, spirits glow.

A serenade of joy and cheer,
With every bloom, the night draws near.
Their chuckles float on gentle breeze,
In the garden, laughter's keys.

The Alchemy of Fragrant Whispers

Whispers weave through fragrant air,
A daffodil recounts a dare.
"Last week I tangled with the breeze,
And almost fell amongst the bees!"

Lemon balm teases with her scent,
While violets plot a merry event.
A rosemary sprig shares her tale,
Of sneaky winds that tried to sail.

Mint and basil hold a jest,
Racing scents, they think they're best.
In this blend of laughs and cheer,
Every bloom has tales to share.

Each petal's secret, humor bright,
Transforming whispers into light.
So here's to blooms that twinkle and wink,
In the alchemy of joy, we think.

Tides of Flora in the Breeze

Flowers dance in winds so bold,
Petals flutter, stories told.
Bees hum tunes of sweet delight,
While bugs in suits have quite a fright.

Lollipops grow on trees, they say,
But only on the fanciest day.
Butterflies wear polka-dot ties,
And gossip with the sneaky flies.

Nature's Symphony of Life

The trees are drummers, leaves a beat,
Squirrels tapping tiny feet.
Birds compose their silly songs,
While frogs croak out the latest wrongs.

Flowers giggle as they bloom,
Chasing away the winter's gloom.
Worms wriggle to a funky tune,
Making earthworms giggle 'neath the moon.

Chronicle of Delicate Traces

In gardens where the veggies play,
Carrots wish they'd never stray.
Radishes wear rosy hats,
While lettuce dreams of dancing cats.

Tomatoes tell tales of great delight,
As sunflowers salute the night.
Cabbages roll with laughter loud,
Joining the merry, leafy crowd.

The Resonance of Fading Blooms

Petals fall like crazy confetti,
Dancing birds invite the pretty.
With each drop a giggle so grand,
We find humor in nature's hand.

The last bloom sighs in silly grace,
Wearing its wilt with a cheeky face.
Nature chuckles as seasons change,
Making even the flowers feel strange.

Moonlit Garden Dreams

Under the moon, the flowers dance,
They whisper secrets, take a chance.
A gnome with glasses starts to creep,
While rabbits yawn and fall asleep.

The stars are laughing, what a sight,
As ladybugs try to take flight.
One trips and tumbles in the grass,
A soft bouquet, he made a pass.

Fireflies buzz with cheeky glee,
Making mischief, just like me.
A bloom declares, 'Let's have a ball!'
The night is young, let's have a draw!

In the garden, dreams take flight,
With silly creatures in the night.
A garden party, all invite,
Come join the fun, till morning light.

Reflections in Dewdrops

On morning's edge, the dewdrops shine,
A raindrop's prank, a little wine.
The petals giggle, full of cheer,
As ants parade, they've found their beer.

Each drop's a mirror, grand and small,
Reflecting antics, one and all.
A snail slips by, with blushing pride,
'Thank you for letting me inside!'

The sun peeks out, the dew takes flight,
While birds in chorus sing with delight.
A butterfly lands, feeling bold,
Wings adorned with tales yet untold.

In every drop, a story spun,
Of silly games and morning fun.
Life's a garden, playful and bright,
In dewdrop laughter, pure delight.

The Lifeblood of Blossoming Souls

In the garden where spirits sing,
With roots entangled, joy does cling.
A daisy winks at a frisky bee,
'You'll never reach my sweet honey!'

A sunflower flaunts its golden crown,
While petunias swirl in fancy gown.
"I'm fabulous!" they chirp with pride,
As bees giggle, swarming wide.

The breeze brings gossip from afar,
With whispers of a distant star.
The roses blush, a moment's tease,
'Oh look, it's April's silly breeze!'

In blooming laughter, the garden thrives,
Each petal bursting, oh how it drives.
The lifeblood flows in every jest,
In this funny realm, we are blessed.

Garden of Sighs

In a garden built of whimsical sighs,
The flowers gossip, they're quite the spies.
A tulip twists with a giggle galore,
'Why not wear perfume? I need a score!'

The willows laugh, their leaves all sway,
While the daisies shine in a cheeky play.
A soft breeze helps them croon and tease,
"Don't take life too serious, just breathe with ease!"

Under the arches, vines climb high,
Listening close to each butterfly.
They sip on nectar, oh so sweet,
While bumblebees dance, oh what a treat!

In this garden where no one cries,
Let's scatter giggles beneath the skies.
With every sigh, a chuckle flies,
In the heart of blooms, laughter lies.

The Dance of the Nature's Brush

In a garden where flowers spin,
Petals twirl in a breezy grin.
Colors clash and tease the bee,
Nature's dance, wild and free.

Butterflies in polka dots,
Giggling while tying knots.
Shadows play tag with the sun,
Who's the champion? Everyone!

The daisies stomp, the roses jive,
All the weeds? They just survive.
With each step, a new surprise,
Nature's waltz, a grand disguise.

Laughter echoes, joy takes flight,
Even the thorns join the delight.
Whirling, twirling, oh what fun,
In the garden where fears are none!

Scented Secrets of the Heart

Whispers float on fragrant air,
Violets gossip without a care.
Roses blush and share a wink,
What's the secret? Mermaid's drink!

Lavender laughs with honey's sweet,
While daisies dance on tiny feet.
Tulips giggle, lilacs sigh,
A symphony of scents nearby.

Petals plot a cheeky scheme,
Beneath the stars, they dream a dream.
Every breeze a secret told,
Heartfelt tales in blooms of gold.

Oh, the romance of the breeze,
Tickling leaves and teasing trees.
In this garden, love's the art,
Scented secrets of the heart!

Beneath the Blossom's Veil

Underneath a sky of pink,
A squirrel stops to laugh and think.
Blossoms drip like melted ice,
Nature's canvas, oh so nice!

Beneath the veil, a world so bright,
Dancing shadows, pure delight.
A ladybug dons a tiny crown,
While butterflies twirl, upside down.

Starlings sing a silly tune,
As the flowers sway, a festive boon.
Crickets chirp as actors play,
Life unfolds in the silliest way.

With every bloom, a chuckle shared,
Joyful moments that none have dared.
Beneath the blossom's cheerful sail,
Let your laughter tell the tale!

The Enigma of the Enchanted Garden

In a garden where oddities bloom,
Porcelain teapots act with zoom.
Gnomes debate who'll dance the best,
While flowers put their skills to test.

Hedgehogs wear their cherry hats,
Bouncing on the backs of gnats.
Whimsical walls that twist and bend,
Around each corner, surprises send.

The fountains giggle, water sprays,
As all the creatures join the craze.
With whispers loud, they plot and scheme,
In this garden, there's no extreme.

What mystery lies in every flower?
Will the petals dance at the hour?
The enigma of this garden so grand,
Leaves us laughing, hand in hand!

Petals in the Breeze

Petals dance like butterflies,
Waving goodbyes to the skies.
They twirl and spin in the sun,
A floral salsa, oh what fun!

Bees buzz by, all in a haste,
Gathering nectar, not one to waste.
A flower sneezes, pollen flies,
And starts a sneeze-off, oh my, oh my!

With a wink, the daisies yell,
"Don't forget us, we play so well!"
The tulips giggle, oh what a sight,
Throwing shade in the warm daylight.

Laughter blooms where petals fall,
Nature's comedy, enchanting all.
As breezes carry whispers near,
A bouquet of joy for all to cheer.

Guardians of the Soft Flora

In a garden where things grow,
Funny creatures put on a show.
Rabbits guard the tender greens,
Sporting hats and silly jeans.

Squirrels chime in, acorns in tow,
Practicing dance moves, high and low.
While flowers giggle, roots in sway,
"They just can't help but frolic all day!"

Sunflowers shout, "Hey! Look at me!"
Striking poses, so wild and free.
Petunias roll on the grassy floor,
As daisies whisper, "Should we join more?"

These soft guardians don't take it serious,
Their antics bloom, wonderfully curious.
With laughter echoing through the night,
The flora reigns in pure delight.

A Symphony of Seasonal Hues

Colors clash in wild embrace,
June blooms bright, a happy face.
Oranges and yellows swirl around,
As petals giggle at the ground.

Breezes hum a funny tune,
Making flowers sway to the moon.
Dandelions join, a wild crew,
Playing tag in shades of blue.

Marigolds laugh, they know the tricks,
While violets whisper their secret picks.
The cherry blossoms join the choir,
All nature's quirks set hearts on fire!

As the seasons come and go,
Floral laughter starts to flow.
A riot of color, a cheerful spike,
In this symphony, we all take a hike.

Memory Fragments in Bloom

Once in spring, we threw a bash,
With forgotten deeds and a vibrant splash.
"Who brought the cake?" we wondered loud,
As we danced around in a colorful crowd.

A daisy held a mic, so bold,
Telling stories both old and gold.
But each funny tale turned slightly askew,
With every giggle, our laughter just grew.

Memory fragments flutter in the air,
Caught in the petals, without a care.
When we forget, the blooms all remember,
Ode to our mishaps in the sun's warm ember.

So here's to the blooms that recall our fun,
Those sunny days where we laughed and ran.
With every laugh, a petal's release,
In this garden of memories, we find our peace.

Harvesting the Essence of Petals

In the garden, giggles bloom,
Petals flew, who can presume?
A bee danced with a silly spin,
Wearing pollen like a grin.

With each snip, we made a mess,
Waltzing flowers in a dress.
Laughter burst like buds in spring,
Harvesting joy, what fun it brings!

Silly hats upon our heads,
Counting blooms like daily spreads.
Who knew petals could be such fun?
A floral race, and we've just begun!

At twilight, friends all gathered tight,
Dancing shadows in the light.
With every petal, mischief grew,
Whispering secrets only we knew.

The Silent Song of Midsummer

In the sun, our laughter floats,
Where the breeze wears funny coats.
Bugs hum tunes, a raucous show,
We join, but dance like we don't know.

A hammock swings, a silly sight,
As friends debate who's out of sight.
Eating ice cream, dripping mess,
Sticky hands but we don't stress.

Chasing shadows, catching light,
In this summer's pure delight.
Petals giggle 'neath our feet,
Summer's song, oh, so sweet!

With water balloons full of dreams,
We launch—what fun, or so it seems!
Each splash a memory we make,
In the warmth, our hearts awake.

Embers of Color in the Courtyard

In the courtyard, colors sway,
With laughter, we paint the day.
A splash of red, a dash of blue,
We throw petals like confetti, too!

Tea parties where nobody sips,
Instead we share our funniest quips.
A parade of hats that none can wear,
Balancing flowers, like we just don't care.

Silly sculptures made of leaves,
Nature giggles as she weaves.
With every bloom and silly dance,
Springtime feels like pure romance.

The sun sets low, shadows will play,
As we waltz the night away.
With colors bright, we bid adieu,
To petals and laughter—what a view!

Petal-Bound Memories

In a scrapbook thick with fun,
A petal tale for everyone.
Flipping through old summer days,
Sticky notes and poppy sprays.

Each memory slips like colored dew,
Caught in laughter, that's our crew.
Bravery where fright should be,
Petal fights, who threw that tree?

We'll dance through pages, twirl and spin,
With every flip, let the giggles begin.
Stories told with petals near,
Whispers of laughter, always dear.

Ink may fade, but smiles remain,
Bound by petals, we'll entertain.
In our hearts, the essence stays,
Silly moments fill our days.

Wisdom Woven in Greenery

In the garden, wisdom bloomed,
A sprout with dreams, quite ill-fumed.
It whispered jokes to the bees,
As they danced on a gentle breeze.

The roses laughed, a thorny crew,
While daisies giggled, bright and new.
The lilacs told tales of the past,
Of leaves that cracked and blossoms cast.

A witty fern waved leaves so proud,
Claiming it was wiser than the crowd.
But the daisies rolled their eyes and grinned,
For nature's laughs had just begun.

So if you stroll through flora's play,
Join in the jokes of the garden's sway.
Where even petals have tales to tell,
Of laughter woven in leafy cells.

The Chronicles of a Budding Soul

Once a bud, full of glee,
Thought it could dance, wild and free.
With a twist and a tumble, it sprouted wide,
But the earth was muddy, and it slipped aside.

A butterfly came, laughing loud,
"Dancing with dirt? You must be proud!"
But the bud just chuckled, not feeling sore,
"Next time, I'll grow near a flower store!"

With sunlight's kiss and raindrop's tease,
The bud grew comfy, among the breeze.
Now it's a bloom, not just a goal,
With funny stories of its budding soul.

So if you see a sprout today,
Don't shy away, just laugh and play.
For every flower has tales to share,
Of setbacks met with light-hearted flair.

Seasons of Reflections and Blossoms

Springtime blooms with chatter and cheer,
While winter mutters that spring is near.
The flowers giggle, a colorful sight,
Saying, "Let's bicker, then hug tight!"

Summer swings with a sunlit swagger,
While autumn rolls in like a gold-leafed dagger.
"Who wore it best?" the petals debate,
As they drop off, it's a shady fate!

In a puddle, reflections do tease,
"Look at us!" they say, "A mirror of ease!"
But even the dullest blooms start to comb,
For every flower dreams of a home.

So here's to the seasons, with laughter galore,
Where petals can dance and joy is a score.
In blooms of all colors, we find our place,
In funny reflections, we all share space.

A Whirlwind of Colors

A whirlwind spins through colorful fields,
As petals swirl in playful shields.
Red giggles with yellow, a sunny affair,
While purple twirls with the winds' wild hair.

"Oh, look at us!" squealed a bright marigold,
"We're the life of the party; let stories unfold!"
As they spun in circles, the daisies joined,
Securing their fame, their laughter coined.

But in the mix, a shy violet came,
Feeling a bit out of the colorful game.
Yet with a breeze, it wiggled and swayed,
Proving that shyness can also parade.

So if a whirlwind catches your eye,
Join the petals, don't let it fly by.
For every hue has a part to play,
In this vibrant dance, come laugh and stay!

Shadows and Petals

In the garden where I tread,
Petals giggle and dance ahead.
Shadows whisper secrets shy,
While bees hum tunes and fly.

A breeze plays tricks, swirls the hue,
Petals spinning, just like you.
I chase them round, what a sight!
Falling flat, now that's delight!

The squirrels laugh, rolling with glee,
As I trip over roots like a bee.
They chitter jokes, I stumble on,
Each petal's path, a comic con!

Yet amidst the laughs and silly falls,
Nature's charm forever calls.
With shadows playing hide and seek,
Petals giggle, making me weak.

The Heartbeat of Green and Pink

In a world of blush and cheer,
Green and pink, my friends draw near.
They jump and bounce with every beat,
Nature's rhythm can't be beat!

A leaf fell down, with quite a flair,
And landed right on my poor hair.
I shook it off, but it had fun,
Dancing on me, oh what a run!

Petals giggle when they're in bloom,
Spreading joy, clearing the gloom.
Each slight breeze they wave hello,
And dance like stars, putting on a show!

The colors burst, a playful sight,
Even raindrops come to delight.
In this garden, life's a spree,
With heartbeats twirling wild and free!

Unraveling Buds in the Breeze

Buds are bursting, springs uncoil,
With laughter carried on the soil.
They peek around with tiny grins,
Inviting sun to join their spins.

The wind arrives with a cheeky bow,
Unraveling buds, it takes a vow.
To swirl and twirl with youthful glee,
As petals fall, they sing to me!

A daisy teased a budding rose,
"Your outfit's nice! Do you pose?"
The rose, embarrassed, turned quite red,
While laughter bloomed, all mischief spread!

In every corner, sprout and play,
Nature's pranks brighten the day.
As buds unfold with joyous ease,
Chasing giggles on the breeze.

Ephemeral Petals and Endless Journeys

Petals drift on paths unknown,
To lands where jokes are freely sown.
They giggle as they twist and weave,
On adventures, oh, you wouldn't believe!

Each drop of rain a splash of fun,
They race like kids, each one a ton!
"To the pond!" one shouts, "To the tree!"
"Let's sail the clouds, just you and me!"

But wait, oh wait, don't miss the show,
They spin around, putting on a glow.
With every flurry, laughter bounds,
In the art of joy, delight surrounds!

Yet time will steal these moments bright,
As petals vanish, out of sight.
But on the breeze, joy's never far,
In ephemeral journeys, we'll always star.

Reverie in a Sea of Flowers

In a garden, blooms align,
Yellow hats and shoes so fine.
Bees buzzing, what a sight,
Dancing petals, pure delight.

Worms wear glasses, quite a show,
Telling secrets none should know.
Squirrels in tuxedos, how absurd,
Cracking jokes with every word.

Roses giggle, daisies snort,
Tulips planning a big, wild sport.
Playing tag among the greens,
With nature's quirks, bursting seams.

Wind whispers tales of carefree days,
Leaves join in with rustling plays.
Laughter echoes through the air,
In this realm, joy's everywhere!

Echoes of the Botanical Heart

In the woods, the trees conspire,
With acorns falling, they conspire.
Mushrooms gossip, roots entwine,
Tales of love and blossoms twine.

A dandelion wears a crown,
While violets spin round and down.
Butterflies in joyful flocks,
Playing chess with rusty clocks.

Singing loud, the flowers gleam,
Every stem speaks of a dream.
Petals giggle with delight,
As crickets dance beneath the light.

Bees are jesters, honey's sweet,
While frogs enjoy a tap dance beat.
Nature's craze, a playful art,
Brings laughter to the botanical heart.

Petals in the Rain

Raindrops fall on cheeky blooms,
Splashing joy in leafy rooms.
A daisy slips, oh what a sight,
Lands in a puddle, full of fright.

Tulips twirl, as raindrops play,
Holding hands in a wet ballet.
Petals giggle, splat—what fun!
Water fights beneath the sun!

Splashing colors, oh what grace,
Sunflowers are in a race.
Chasing droplets down the hill,
Who knew rain could thrill?

With laughter loud, the garden sings,
Petals dancing on their springs.
Puddles echo endless glee,
Nature's party, wild and free!

Whispers of Spring Blossoms

In the meadow, whispers rise,
Flowers gossip 'neath blue skies.
Tulips whisper, 'Guess who's here?'
A bumblebee, with no fear!

Roses blushing, giggling shy,
Petals fluttering, oh my, my!
Violets cheer and daisies clap,
While squirrels nap, what a map!

Songbirds croon with merry hearts,
Nature's stage and all its parts.
Crickets chirp a joyful tune,
Beneath the light of a lazy moon.

Spring's confetti fills the air,
Every bloom has tales to share.
In laughter loud, their secrets hum,
A garden laugh—oh, spring's so fun!

A Tapestry of Floral Stories

In a garden where flowers conspire,
Petals gossip, each tale a choir.
A daisy winks, a rose rolls her eyes,
As tulips laugh at tall grass's lies.

Butterflies swoon in a floral cafe,
Serving nectar, the drink of the day.
Bees buzz tales of sweet summer flings,
While sunflowers dance, ignoring their strings.

A gnome listens in, with a grin on his face,
Tickled by petals in their merry race.
But beware of the weeds that lurk in the shade,
With their pranks and mischief, all fun is delayed.

So join in the laughter, come see what's in store,
Where blooms are the storytellers, forevermore.
With humor and joy, this garden will thrive,
In a tapestry woven where friendship's alive.

When Blossoms Weep at Dusk

As the sun sets low and the shadows creep,
The flowers sigh, and some start to weep.
Laughter turns quiet, as petals do frown,
In the twilight whispers, a soft, gentle gown.

A clumsy bee stumbles, buzzing his fears,
While daisies brush off the rain with their tears.
A pig in the mud, dreaming of flight,
Makes the day's end feel comically right.

In the hush of the dusk, a rose gives a yawn,
While phlox spins tales of love and of dawn.
They giggle and shuffle, despite their sad fate,
Finding joy even late, it's never too late.

So when blossoms weep, do not shed a tear,
For laughter still lingers, and smiles draw near.
In the dark, they'll plot their bright merry jest,
As night wraps the garden in a velvet vest.

In the Embrace of Nature's Palette

In a riot of colors, the blooms start to play,
Dancing together, brightening the day.
A marigold tripped on a jolly old vine,
While violets snickered, "Now that's quite divine!"

The daisies wear shades of the silliest hue,
And tell the tall reeds, "Join in; it's true!"
With tulips that twist and daffodils sing,
Creating a ruckus, oh what joy they bring!

A rainbow appears, as butterflies swoon,
Underneath all these blossoms, a lighthearted tune.
Roses share secrets, as laughter unfolds,
In nature's embrace, no drama but bolds.

So let's paint our lives like this garden so bright,
With humor and colors, a whimsical sight.
In the embrace of the blooms, let's joyfully trot,
In this marvelous palette, we find our sweet spot.

Tales from the Garden of Solitude

In the corners of quiet, where whispers collide,
Flowers share tales, where secrets abide.
A lone peony ponders, perplexed by the sun,
While the ivy giggles, "You're still number one!"

A fern feels forgotten, in shadows so deep,
Yet dreams of grand stories begin to creep.
With snickers from bark and a sly nod from grass,
In the solitude's heart, the joy comes to pass.

The tulip throws shade, but deep down it knows,
Amidst all the silence, the laughter still grows.
They dance through the night, under starlit repose,
In a garden of solitude, where humor just flows.

So come join the party where quiet blooms loud,
In the tales of the garden, let's laugh and feel proud.
For even in stillness, the fun finds a way,
In the thicket of petals, let's frolic and play.

The Poetry of Pollen

In the garden, bees do dance,
Chasing blooms with swift romance.
Pollen clings to every nose,
That's how garden mischief grows.

Sneezing fits, oh what a sight,
Allergic rhymes take flight at night.
Flowers giggle as they sway,
'Is that nectar, or just hay?'

Pollen poems, sticky lines,
Written on the backs of pines.
Nature's jest, so sweetly spun,
Who knew sneezes could be fun?

Buzzing humor in the air,
Allergy season, handle with care!
Yet in the mess of these sniffs and snorts,
Laughter blooms in nature's courts.

Enchanted by Blossoms

In a meadow, flowers prance,
Swirling petals, nature's dance.
A dandelion in disguise,
Proclaims, 'I'm the fairest of the guys!'

A tulip tops the others tall,
But sneaks a peek, and starts to fall.
'Don't mind me,' she laughs so bright,
'Just practicing for my flight!'

Roses boast of fragrant charms,
While daisies wave their little arms.
But bees roll their eyes and sigh,
'Got pollen? Pass it by!'

Each bloom adds more to the show,
As the sun dips low and glows.
In this circus of sweet scents,
Every petal's laughter repents.

Lament of the Withering Week

Monday blooms, then starts to fade,
A droopy petal's masquerade.
Tuesday's still in bed too late,
Whining 'why must I participate?'

Hump day hits, the blooms go wild,
"Oh look, I'm just a garden child!"
But Thursday brings the dreaded shoo,
'Please, no mowing—let us stew!'

By Friday, petals plot escape,
'Let's join a flowery landscape!'
But plans go south on Saturday,
When weeds crash in to start the fray.

Then Sunday reigns with soft regrets,
A week of mirth, but no hot bets.
Withered smiles in flower beds,
Dreaming blooms rest their weary heads.

Soft Whispers Amidst Flowering

The violets gossip in the breeze,
"Did you hear about those bees?"
With roses blushing, thorns on guard,
"Don't get too close, their buzz is hard!"

Lilies giggle, petals shake,
"Let's pretend we're no mistake!"
But tulips beam, curl up with pride,
"Let's start a flower's joy-filled ride!"

Underneath the sun's warm gaze,
Petal whispers weave through days.
Inane jokes flower in the air,
Nature's fun, with nary a care.

Dew drops laugh, give blooms a soak,
"Here's to flowers' freshest joke!"
In this garden, smiles take flight,
Whispers dance, such pure delight.

Bridging the Seasons with Petals

A winter bloom can cause a fuss,
While summer bees compete on buses.
Spring's laughter fills the air so light,
While autumn's drama takes to flight.

Petals dance from branch to ground,
As squirrels scold, quite mirror-bound.
Time hops like a jolly frog,
Bounding through the morning fog.

Each season throws a silly hat,
They giggle with the sneaky cat.
Nature's pranks, a comical flare,
Life in flowers, a playful affair.

Floral Testaments to Time

Roses wear the crown of years,
Tulips chuckle, shedding tears.
Daisy chains of shiny dreams,
Stickiness from honey seams.

Sunflowers flirt with every glance,
Cacti steal the afternoon dance.
Petal whispers, tales so wild,
A garden's jest, nature's child.

Lilies learn to play charades,
Petunias join in quirky raids.
With every twist, the colors sing,
A timeless game, a joyful fling.

Adrift in Petal Dust

In a cloud of petals, I float,
Dizzy from the floral boat.
Bees buzz by, a merry crew,
Chasing skies of baby blue.

A dandy lion jokes with glee,
While trees play hide and seek with me.
Petal dust, just like confetti,
Makes every moment feel quite heady.

Wind-swept giggles wrap the air,
A flower crown, beyond compare.
With laughter loud and bright display,
Petal dust takes cares away.

A Symphony Beneath the Leafy Canopy

Beneath the leaves, the band begins,
With rustling roots and tiny sins.
A woodpecker keeps time with taps,
While squirrels provide the funny snaps.

Mushrooms wear their hats with pride,
While ferns play peek-a-boo, they hide.
The canopy, a vibrant chart,
Each petal's note, a work of art.

As laughter echoes through the glade,
Every blossom, a serenade.
A symphony of silly glee,
Underneath the leafy spree.

Portraits of the Blooming Heart

In a garden where flowers chatter,
Green thumbs join in the playful clatter.
A rose tells jokes, making daisies cheer,
While tulips giggle, drawing near.

The sun struts in, a bright-faced chap,
As bumblebees buzz a silly rap.
Petals dance like they've lost their minds,
In this wild garden, joy unwinds.

Yet in the shade, the shy buds peep,
Whispering secrets that make us weep.
A cactus dons shades, looking so cool,
While violets plot, playing it shrewd.

Underneath the moon, the night laughs loud,
With fireflies winking, they form a crowd.
Together they sing, a merry tune,
In this bloom, hearts rise like balloons.

A Serenade of Scent and Shade

Petunias strum on guitar strings,
While lilacs hum of silly things.
The air is thick with laughter's scent,
In this floral realm, fun's never spent.

A sunflower twirls in a wobbly spin,
As marigolds cheer for the silly win.
Butterflies flutter with flapping grace,
Dancing around in this carefree space.

There's mischief lurking in the blooms,
As dandelions puff out their plumes.
With every breeze, a ticklish tease,
Nature's jesters bring us to our knees.

Even the wind joins the merry song,
Blowing along, it just can't go wrong.
New fragrances blend, a lively parade,
In this joyful garden, shade never fades.

Nature's Timeless Embrace

A squirrel juggling acorns with flair,
While birds chirp gossip up in the air.
The trees chuckle, their leaves in ballet,
As nature winks, ready to play.

Tadpoles splash in a puddle with glee,
Creating ripples for all to see.
Amidst the blooms, a convention of bees,
Debating the best nectar with an expertise.

With ants on parade, all in a line,
They march with purpose, perfectly fine.
A rose dreams big, wishes to fly,
While daisies giggle, "We can give it a try!"

Under the sun, where laughter ignites,
The wildflowers gather for playful delights.
In nature's arms, where all feels right,
Every day is a comical sight.

Blooming Echoes of Memory

In the garden of jokes, where laughter's loud,
Pansies cover their smiles with a proud shroud.
Tulips recall when they played in the rain,
While giggling violets share tales of pain.

"Remember the snow?" says a bold petunia,
"Goodbye, winter! We're back in our junior!"
A daisy grins, it knows the game,
Recall of the past is never the same.

Then comes the sun, with mischief instilled,\nChasing off clouds, every frown is thrilled.
Bright petals burst into fits of delight,
While shadows pull pranks under moonlight.

With echoes of laughter swirling the air,
In this blooming world, all is laid bare.
Every scent tells a story, unique and bright,
As memories bloom in the soft, warm light.

Whispers of Petal Dreams

In a garden of giggles, blooms shyly sway,
With petals that dance on a sunny ballet.
Ladybugs gossip on leaves oh so green,
As daisies chuckle with a sly little gleam.

The roses wear secrets, in hues bright and bold,
While violets giggle, their stories unfold.
A sunflower snores in the midday sun's heat,
While tulips are plotting a wild flower feat.

The wind tells a joke to the trees all around,
They rustle and chuckle, a funny sound.
Each bloom holds a riddle, so odd yet so grand,
In this playful garden, where joy is unplanned.

So let us gather, with laughter our theme,
In the color-rich world of petal-filled dreams.
For nature's the jester, crafting roots deep and wide,
In the whimsical realm where delight cannot hide.

Secrets Beneath the Bloom

Beneath every blossom, a secret takes flight,
A tulip's confession in the soft moonlight.
With petals that whisper a tale of their own,
Who knew that such gossip in gardens has grown?

The daisies are plotting a prank on the bees,
While chasing the shadows, they giggle with ease.
Roses blush deeply at a rumor they hear,
That dandelions wish to grow tall without fear.

A secret so juicy that the heat makes it ripe,
The lilies all chuckle and munch on some hype.
They wink at the grass as it wiggles with glee,
In the land of the blooms where all's silly and free.

So next time you wander where laughter might flow,
Seek secrets in petals, let your worries go.
For nature's old stories are always retold,
In the garden where wisdom and whimsy unfold.

The Elegance of Silent Blooms

Silent blooms linger, with elegance grand,
Yet giggles erupt, can you understand?
The peonies ponder the tales they spin,
While orchids are plotting a party within.

Each stem has a story, a dance in the breeze,
Cactus in sneakers perplexed as they tease.
A daisy finds joy in a bumblebee's wink,
While pansies concoct a wild, joyful drink.

The quietest petals have fun up their sleeves,
Spreading light laughter like soft autumn leaves.
In the ballet of blooms, where nothing is shy,
The elegance whispers with twinkling eye.

So come join the party, in gardens divine,
Where silence erupts and the flowers align.
With elegance dancing, and petals in cheer,
In the world of the blooms, there's nothing to fear.

Garden of Forgotten Echoes

In the garden of echoes, where memories sprout,
An old sunflower sings what it's all about.
The lilacs remember those jests from the past,
While roses are blushing, their giggles amassed.

Forget-me-nots chuckle at tales of yore,
As daisies do cartwheels, then tumble and soar.
With each little breeze, the laughter persists,
In shadows of petals, where joy can't be missed.

An echoing chorus of whispers takes flight,
With marigolds dancing, a comical sight.
In this garden of laughter, where secrets abound,
The blooms paint a canvas with joy all around.

So let every flower, with stories to share,
Remind us of echoes that linger in air.
For in the garden's embrace, with laughter we see,
The magic of blooms is forever carefree.

The Secrets Weaved in Stems

In a garden where petals giggle,
Stems hold jokes, that make us wiggle.
The gardener whispers, 'What's that knack?'
'Why do blossoms never hold back?'

With roots that dance in a soil so deep,
They gossip secrets, not meant to keep.
A tulip winks, while daisies snort,
'Why did the rose go to court?'

A daffodil's singing, 'Not-so-secret!'
While sunflowers grin—what a wild feat!
Do colors choose, or come out at night?
In a riot of hues, they start a fight!

So next time you stroll past the blooms in cheer,
Remember, they're plotting and partying here.
In every little stem, a tale is spun,
A floral comedy, just for fun!

Fragrant Stories Underfoot

Down by the roots where the daisies play,
Concrete jungles whisper, 'Sway, sway, sway.'
With thyme rolling dice and mint giggling loud,
They plot mischievous tricks beneath the shroud.

'What if we throw a garden rave?'
Said the bold little weed, so brazen and brave.
'Let's call the insects, and top it with dew!
We'll dance till the sun rises bright and new!'

The roses blush at the noise they make,
While violets chuckle, 'For goodness' sake!'
A worm in a tux prances by with charm,
'You're all invited—come on, don't be alarmed!'

So next time you walk on green growth and dirt,
Listen closely to stories, or you might get hurt.
For in each little petal, an adventure awaits,
In the fragrant depths where humor elates!

Cartography of the Floral World

On a map of blossoms where petals chart,
Each tulip marked with a funny part.
'Here lies the rose with a prickly crown,
Avoid her thorns — she won't let you down!'

By the pond, under willows that sway,
The lily pads whisper, 'Join us today!'
'A treasure of stinkbugs is waiting near,'
As frogs play hopscotch, shedding all fear.

The ferns wave flags, while daisies decree,
'Let's draw our future, carefree as can be.'
With watercolor skies and muddy old paths,
They laugh at the maps drawn in heartfelt drafts.

So lift up your gaze to the floral spread,
Where petals and laughter dance overhead.
With quirks and antics, they map out delight,
In a world so funny, everything feels right!

Timeless Tales of the Flora

In the blooms of time, where legends unfold,
Each petal is grounded in stories retold.
The sunflower speaks of its golden cheer,
'They plant me for smiles and lend me an ear!'

Lilies debate who's the fairest of all,
While bees in tuxedos come shimmy and crawl.
The vibrant zinnia jokes with the breeze,
'What's a flower's favorite game? Oh, it's frisbees!'

A dandelion wishes with puffs all around,
Carefree and funny, it frolics unbound.
With wishes like fireworks flying so high,
It twirls with the clouds, each dream like a sigh.

So remember the garden, where laughter convenes,
In timeless tales woven through petals and greens.
Each flower a jest, each leaf a new turn,
In the land of the flora, there's always more to learn!

A Dance of Color and Fragrance

Petals swirling in a jest,
Colors laughing at the sun,
Fragrant friends in bloom's embrace,
Join the dance, it's so much fun!

Bumblebees in fancy suits,
Buzzing jokes from flower to flower,
Their tiny feet like tap shoes clap,
In this garden of pure power!

Sunbeams play a game of tag,
While shadows hide in giggles,
Every plant's a comedian,
Bouncing jokes with tiny wiggles!

Oh, the blooms have tales to tell,
When the breezes start to tease,
Each petal's laugh is sweet and bright,
In the garden of such ease!

Threads of Nature's Tapestry

Weaving laughter in the vines,
Nature's needles all in play,
Sunlight shines on threads of green,
Stitching joy in bright array.

Butterflies with flair abound,
Dancing on the warp and weft,
A silk parade, all polished up,
Nature's banter, love's own theft!

Raindrops giggle on the leaves,
Sewing kisses as they fall,
Woven jokes in every drop,
Nature's humor, fun for all!

At twilight, the loom unwinds,
Stars come out, a shimmering show,
In this fabric, joy entwined,
Nature's tale will giggle and glow!

The Elegance Within Blossoms

Oh, what grace in petals' prance,
Bowing low when breezes call,
Each bloom knows its dance and stance,
Whispering elegance to all.

Stems do salsa, leaves will twirl,
Flowers flirt with passing bees,
In this garden, colors swirl,
Nature's humor brings us ease!

Morning dew like a diamond laugh,
Sparkling jokes that lift our hearts,
Blossoms show their bright path,
In this play, each joy imparts.

With petals soft, we tease the day,
With every bloom, a chuckle flies,
In elegance, we find the play,
Nature's laughter never dies!

Hushed Conversations of the Meadow

In the meadow, whispers rise,
Flowers gossip in the breeze,
Their secrets shared with passing flies,
Underneath the swaying trees.

Laughter lingers in the air,
Dandelions puff their dreams,
Giggling with a breeze that's rare,
Nature's humor in soft beams.

Tulips gossip in bold hues,
"Did you see that butterfly?"
With every sway, their tales amuse,
In laughter's grasp, they fly high.

Even shadows chime in, too,
Beneath the dance of light and shade,
In this meadow, fun is true,
As nature's laughter will not fade!

The Soliloquy of Blooming Hearts

In a garden where laughter thrives,
Petals gossip about silly jives,
A bee trips over its own black feet,
While the daisies laugh, oh what a feat!

Rose whispers secrets, oh so juicy,
While the tulips giggle, feeling choosy,
The sun plays tag with clouds up above,
As weeds declare they're worthy of love!

Petunias waltz in a colorful riot,
While lilacs argue, 'We're the quiet!'
Each flower thinks it wears the crown,
While the wind dances, swirling them down.

So here's to blooms with stories to share,
In this wacky garden, none have a care,
When petals unroll and laugh in delight,
It's a party of colors, oh what a sight!

Reflections of a Fragile Spring

A quiet pond, where frogs tell their tales,
About flying ducks and their silly fails,
The lotus rolls its eyes at the fuss,
While the fish just giggle, 'No need to rush!'

Buds peek out, unsure of their fate,
A bloom turns to its neighbor, 'Let's celebrate!'
With awkward stretches, they wobble and sway,
Making butterflies laugh, 'What a display!'

Dewdrops sit on leaves, feeling so bold,
They whisper secrets that never get told,
While the breeze chuckles, playing with hair,
A parade of petals, all dancing with flair!

Oh, fragile spring, with your jokes in the air,
Your humor brings joy, light, and sweet care,
So let's welcome each bloom with a grin,
For nature's laughter makes the heart spin!

The Dance of Sunlit Leaves

Leaves rustle softly, sharing a jest,
As the sunlight gives them its warm zest,
A leaf with flair does a twirl and glide,
While its buddy whispers, 'You're quite the pride!'

A squirrel on a branch, full of wild dreams,
Pretends to be serious, or so it seems,
While the acorns below roll their eyes in disdain,
Claiming they'll stick to their oak-ly terrain!

The dancing shadows create quite a scene,
As the blossoms tease, 'Look at us, so serene!'
A gust of wind brings a cheeky bouquet,
Swirling around, making all the leaves sway!

So let the leaves spin in this grand ballet,
While the forest chuckles, 'What a fine day!'
With nature's humor, life's always a spree,
In a symphony of laughter, wild and free!

Eulogy of the Fading Blossom

Gather round, dear friends, hear the tale,
Of a lovely bloom that set sail,
Its petals gently trembled with glee,
As the sun whispered, 'Just wait and see!'

But one cheeky breeze had other ideas,
It swept through the garden with ticklish sneezes,
The flower gasped, 'Oh dear, not today!'
As it waved goodbye in a flamboyant way!

With a wink to the roses, it took its last bow,
While the daisies laughed, 'You're a star, oh wow!'
Petals drift down, a confetti parade,
Celebrating the life of the bloom that had played!

So let this be a lesson, dear blooms everywhere,
Life's funny moments are the best to share,
In the garden of giggles, we all find our way,
Even fading blossoms can still greet the day!

Requiem for Fallen Petals

Oh petals drop, like candy rain,
Each one whispers, "What a pain!"
The breeze sighs with a chuckle near,
"Guess that's nature's way of beer!"

A dance of colors lost from trees,
The ground is dressed in flowery tease.
"You're late for brunch!" the flowers cry,
As bees buzz by with a wink and sigh.

They gather round a vibrant grill,
Spilling nectar, what a thrill!
A picnic here, yet petals weep,
For salads made of blooms that sleep.

So raise a glass to fallen friends,
Toast to petals, where joy transcends.
For every bloom that meets its fate,
A laugh or two we must create.

Where Flora Meets the Soul

In gardens deep, where giggles sprout,
Where daisies prance and tulips shout.
"Why so serious?" the roses tease,
As sunbeams play among the leaves.

A fern leans close, "Let's start a band!"
With bumblebees as our rockin' stand.
"But who's the drummer?" a daffodil asks,
While the violets plot floral tasks.

The chatter buzzes, a wild affair,
"A shrub can't dance, that's just not fair!"
With petals fluffed, they spin and whirl,
Nature's stage, a floral twirl.

So let your leaves hang loose and low,
Join the romp where laughter flows.
In every bud, a spark lives bold,
A garden's heart, a sight to behold.

Chronicles Written in Floral Ink

In petals soft, the stories bloom,
Of stalks and stems in their sweet gloom.
"Why don't we write?" the orchids cheered,
While lilies blushed, their fates appeared.

A quill made of a twig, how neat!
With pollen ink that smells so sweet.
"But careful, friends, don't spill too much!"
A daisy squealed, "I'm not a crutch!"

On parchment leaf, their tales unfold,
Of wind and sun—their grip so bold.
They pen their dreams of sunny skies,
While bunnies hop to read and sighs.

So gather close, let laughter weave,
In floral lore, you won't believe.
With every line, a petal grins,
Chronicles where the giggle spins.

The Unfolding of Celestial Blooms

When twilight calls, the blooms awake,
With giggles soft, they bend and shake.
"Is it a party?" the stars will wink,
As flowers sip on nectar drink.

A petal in a party hat,
Swaying 'round with a bouncy cat.
"Tonight we dine on starlit cakes!"
They laugh and dance, each movement quakes.

The night unfolds in shades so bright,
While crickets join in pure delight.
"Let's twirl like dandelions soft!"
And tremble 'neath the moon aloft.

With celestial friends, the blooms ascend,
In laughter's arms, their joys extend.
For every night of twinkling light,
Floral dreams take flight, out of sight!

Tides of Floral Memory

In a garden, flowers dance and sway,
They giggle and whisper, in their own way.
The daisies shout, "We're the real stars!"
While tulips wear funny hats from Mars!

Bees buzzing like they're in a race,
Chasing petals with such a silly grace.
The roses just roll their eyes with glee,
"We're all the same in this floral spree!"

Blooming Shadows and Sunlight

Sunlight tickles leaves with a bright laugh,
While shadows play peek-a-boo on their path.
A daffodil dons a yellow cape,
Claiming it can fly, oh what a shape!

Petals prancing like dancers on a stage,
Whispering secrets from flower to sage.
Lilies wear sunglasses, oh so cool,
While tulips join in, breaking every rule!

The Language of Velvet Leaves

Velvet leaves gossip under the trees,
Saying, "Did you hear? The daisies tease!"
They claim a squirrel stole their best bloom,
While robins chuckle, filling the room.

The ferns tell tales of summer's delight,
While sunsets paint them in rosy light.
Every leaf whispers a story so sly,
In this world where flowers never say die!

Echoes in the Greenhouse

Inside the greenhouse, laughter takes flight,
As orchids debate who's the most bright.
A cactus speaks up, with a prickly grin,
"I may be sharp, but I still fit in!"

The pots are a riot, full of delight,
With ferns and ivy in a playful fight.
A geranium winks, with a cheeky sway,
"Let's start a party, hip-hip-hooray!"

www.ingramcontent.com/pod-product-compliance
Lightning Source LLC
Chambersburg PA
CBHW071823160426
43209CB00003B/183